WONDERFUL
WORDS FOR LIFE

Bob Gentzler

WESTBOW
PRESS®
A DIVISION OF THOMAS NELSON
& ZONDERVAN

WestBow Press books may be ordered through booksellers or by contacting:

WestBow Press
A Division of Thomas Nelson & Zondervan
1663 Liberty Drive
Bloomington, IN 47403
www.westbowpress.com
844-714-3454

Scripture taken from the King James Version of the Bible.

ISBN: 978-1-6642-4160-2 (sc)
ISBN: 978-1-6642-4162-6 (hc)
ISBN: 978-1-6642-4161-9 (e)

Library of Congress Control Number: 2021915272

Print information available on the last page.

WestBow Press rev. date: 07/31/2021

First, to my children. Rob, your talents will take you everywhere you want to go with God's blessing. Billy, God loves you and has great plans for your life. Madison, God has set His angels all around you. Aim high. You will not fall. Jamison, my Jami, Jesus loves you. This I know!

And to my wife, Fran, who supports me and believes in me. This book is for you, for with God, all things are possible! Love endures all things.

CONTENTS

INTRODUCTION

People are drowning! They are drowning in a sea of uncertainty. We are being told that our Bibles are no longer the Word of God. *Truth* is now negotiable. Many confessing Christians have Bibles that are not being read, and unfortunately, those Bibles are only collecting dust. Biblical illiteracy is destroying the church. How can we truly know God if we fail to read about Him within the pages of His Word?

Wonderful Words for Life addresses the many areas of concern for today's Christian believer. Has failure left you shipwrecked on an island of despair? Has seeking forgiveness eluded you? Is there someone whom *you* still have not forgiven? Is it yourself? Are you aware of what you should bring to worship? Who or what is the Holy Spirit? False teachers are all around us. Are you able to recognize them? Can you trust the Bible?

All of those topics are addressed in God's Word. Wonderful words for healing, for comfort, and for hope can be found throughout the Bible—and so much more! You don't need to purchase any self-help books. God has all the answers for you in his Word, the Bible!

Are you keeping your eyes on Jesus? Life is not a game, so why are you keeping score? How do I get my children interested in church? Sin, the forbidden topic! Why am I so angry? Anxiety is weighing me down!

I have been teaching God's Word for twenty-eight years. God enlisted me to be a teacher's helper for my son's fifth-grade Sunday school class. This sounded harmless enough. *Enlisted* is the correct word to describe what I had signed up for. It was truly warfare! On this first day of Sunday school, I was informed that I would not be a teacher's helper; I *was* the teacher! As I nervously gathered the handouts for the week's Bible lesson, I quickly realized I was in trouble. As fast as I handed out the materials, the children converted them into airplanes, which they launched over the partitions toward the other classes. I couldn't wait for the class to end.

After a soul-searching week of prayer, I planned a new strategy. The next Sunday, I set aside the lesson handouts. I quickly took attendance and asked the children to help me with today's lesson materials, which were plywood, paint, staples, and other building supplies. They were all focused, waiting on my every word! I told them that they were going to build Noah's ark for the younger classes to use in their upcoming play. As I directed each of them, I taught them the Bible lesson, and they learned.

I have taught Sunday school for various age groups. I am currently teaching the adult Sunday school class at our church in Linwood Heights. I have created our own vacation Bible school curriculum for themes such as creation, love, Bible heroes, and angels.

We enjoyed a very successful youth activity, using the theme of *Raiders of the Lost Ark*. Using a Styrofoam chest, painted gold with rings and poles, we brought real excitement to our Bible quest. Using maps and Bible riddles, we had the children search for the hidden ark. Never tell me the Bible is boring!

I have taught Bible lessons online across the world. My oldest member, being eighty-six, was also my most distant member, as she lived in Queensland, Australia! I taught under the pseudonym "Chris Ed," which was short for *Christian education*. I am currently teaching Bible lessons about the Gospels. I have several members who have completed more than sixty lessons, working at their own pace.

I have also preached several sermons in two different Methodist churches. I have been a Christian education chairman, a lay-leader, a Christ Servant minister, a youth activity planner, a teacher for children's church, and Bible thespian! "I love to tell the story."

You will feel renewed and refreshed when you read the Bible verses that I have included in my text. Each one clearly defines God's desire for our lives. The Bible is meant to bring you closer to God. It is time to take an honest look at your life, addressing those areas that have been neglected. *Wonderful Words for Life* will encourage you to be the Christian God wants you to be!

Blessings to you!

CHAPTER ONE

Keep Your Eyes on Jesus

Sing them over again to me, wonderful words of life, let me more of their beauty see, wonderful words of life, words of life and beauty teach me faith and duty.

Beautiful words, wonderful words, wonderful words of life Beautiful words, wonderful words, wonderful words of life.

This hymn, written by Phillip P. Bliss in 1874, is one of my favorites. He was a singing evangelist who traveled through the Midwest and the South, leading music at revival meetings at the urging of Dwight L. Moody. I love to sing this hymn as often as I can. Even my children know the melody and his words.

The words that I read from my King James Bible are indeed wonderful words of life. That is why I am writing this book—to impress upon the reader the importance, the splendor, and the truth that is recorded within the pages of God's Word. For we read in John 6:68, "Then Simon Peter answered him, Lord, to whom shall we go? Thou hast the words of eternal life."

God wants the best for us, and for every situation in life, God lights the path! Proverbs 3:5–6 tells us,

> Trust in the Lord with all thine heart, and lean not unto thine own understanding. In all thy ways acknowledge him, and he shall direct thy paths.

The word translated as "trust" means to lie helpless, facedown. It pictures an obedient servant waiting for his master's command. If our trust in God is truthful, it must be given in its entirety. "With all thine heart" requires it!

Life is full of wonderful adventures and opportunities. You can dedicate yourself to any purpose you wish. Many spend a lifetime practicing tirelessly to become musicians, artists, athletes, dancers, or other types of performers. Then there are the teachers, writers, pastors, doctors, nurses, technicians, carpenters, electricians, plumbers, firefighters, and police officers. All of them study countless hours to hone their skills and live their dreams. The lists go on and on, proving we have the capacity to become most anything we desire.

A famous quote from the great sculptor Michelangelo speaks

to what focus and dedication to a chosen craft look like. "I saw the angel in the marble and carved until I set him free."

God has equipped humankind with great potential. Whether or not we waste this potential or utilize it is up to us.

One of the things that seems to hold us back from achieving our goals and aspirations is taking our eyes off our target. I cannot overstate the importance of this flaw.

Everyone knows that Jesus walked on water! But what many people miss is that Peter did likewise, albeit briefly. In the account found in Matthew 14:26–31, we read,

> And when the disciples saw him walking on the sea, they were troubled, saying, "It is a ghost;" and they cried out for fear. But straightway Jesus spoke unto them, saying, "Be of good cheer, it is I; be not afraid." And Peter answered him and said, "Lord, if it be thou, bid me come unto thee on the water." And he said, "Come." And when Peter was come down out of the boat, he walked on the water, to go to Jesus. But when he saw the wind boisterous, he was afraid; and beginning to sink, he cried, saying, "Lord, save me." And immediately Jesus stretched forth his hand, and caught him, and said unto him, "O thou of little faith, why didst thou doubt?"

Well, I think we know why Peter doubted. He took his eyes off Jesus and allowed the turbulence of his surroundings to sink his faith. He was indeed walking on water, just as Christ had done, but his thoughts and focus turned to his surroundings, inviting fear to ruin the moment.

Why is it so hard for us to stay focused? Why do we sometimes lose track of our goals? There are many distractions that we need to deal with in life. Some of these are unavoidable, such as unforeseen circumstances. These bumps in the road can be simply annoyances that we have to deal with, or they can become fracturing halts to our progress. It depends on how we react to the bump.

Pastor Charles R. Swindoll has this to say about those bumps we might encounter: "Life is 10 percent what happens to you, and 90 percent how you react to it."

Those are profound words. It is how we react to things that determines our actions. Will we react to an unkind criticism from a stranger, a friend, or a family member with disdain or see it as an opportunity to correct a flaw and better ourselves?

It is far too easy to feel hurt and discouraged when we hear something negative. In these circumstances, we see how much positive reinforcement does for building up confidence in one's abilities. As Christians reflecting the love of God, we should in every circumstance be encouraging. Tearing people down is easy, while encouraging them can be life altering! A kind word is always much more welcome and beneficial.

Like Peter, we cannot afford to take our eyes off Jesus. John 15:5 reminds us, "I am the vine, ye are the branches." We get our strength from Him. We cannot bear good fruits if we lose this connection. And we cannot be all God intends us to be if we are severed from the vine.

Are you looking at the boisterous winds of this world as Peter did? You need not be. We find wonderful words for life in Colossians 3:1–2.

> If ye, then, be risen with Christ, seek those things
> which are above, where Christ sitteth on the right
> hand of God. Set your affection on things above,
> not on things on the earth.

Paul is reminding us of the lordship of Christ and that true believers have been buried and raised again with Christ! This truth testifies that we have died to our old life and its sinful ways. We are to set our minds on things above because that is where Jesus is.

As followers of Christ, we need to stay focused on the truth of His word. This can only come about if you regularly feed your soul by reading the scriptures. It will prepare you for whatever chaos comes your way. Jesus echoes this idea in Matthew 4:4. "But he answered and said, It is written, Man shall not live by bread alone, but by every word that proceedeth out of the mouth of God."

There will always be days when the "winds" and "waves" will seem insurmountable. But know this: you are not alone! Staying focused on Christ will require you to eliminate the distractions that are keeping you from Him. Satan lives in the distractions of life. This is where he does his best work of trying to keep us out of the light and wandering off the path God has laid before us. The apostle Peter says it best in 1 Peter 5:8, "Be sober, be vigilant, because your adversary, the devil, like a roaring lion walketh about, seeking whom he may devour." Be prepared for his deceptive diversions.

Finding time to connect with Jesus is paramount in our Christian life. We can accomplish this daily by starting to listen to praise music during the week. Waiting for a Sunday-morning pick-me-up from familiar praise songs or favorite hymns is not enough. We need to continually hear the words of these songs that praise God while lifting our own spirits. You will notice a calming peace come over you when you more regularly hear the reassuring messages contained in those trusted Christian hymns.

You can also join a Bible study. Anything you can do to ensure that you are opening God's Word on a regular basis is beneficial! At the very least, get one of those devotional booklets that offer a scripture for every day of the year. You will be surprised when, before long, you discover favorite verses and are able to commit them to memory. Jesus encourages us in John 8:31–32,

> Then said Jesus to those Jews who believed on him, If ye continue in my word, then are ye my disciples indeed; And ye shall know the truth, and the truth shall make you free.

Pray. Pray in the morning, pray at lunch, and pray every night before you go to sleep. This one thing is the most undervalued aspect of the Christian life. We need to commit to a more vibrant prayer life since we are encouraged to boldly come before God. Hebrews 4:16 declares, "Let us, therefore, come boldly unto the throne of grace, that we may obtain mercy, and find grace to help in time of need."

This is one of those verses that should delight your heart. It assures us that we do not have to cower anxiously when we come to God in prayer. He knows all things, and He can read the thoughts of our hearts. All is laid bare before His magnificent presence! Like a loving father, God welcomes us with open arms, eager to provide for us all that He has promised.

We live in a stormy, turbulent world. Howling winds of change threaten us from all directions. Crashing waves of uncertainty rule the day. But we can brave the storm because we are not alone. Our Savior is right there with us, waiting for us to call His name and cry, "Save me, Lord!"

It is time for you to step out of the boat!

CHAPTER TWO

Life Is Not a Game, So Why Are We Keeping Score?

Obviously, no one really looks at life as a game. It is obvious, isn't it? Even though we may have been systematically programmed since birth to react in certain ways to sights, sounds, smells, and such, life remains anything but a game.

From the moment we get up until the moment we lay down our heads to rest, we are inundated with sense-stimulating imagery. And like sponges, we soak up every bit of them!

You really cannot avoid them. There are a vast number of talented *influencers* making sure you do not miss a thing! And they use every type of media to get your attention. If Satan held an earthly job, he would excel in the advertisement industry, because of its deceptive and alluring attributes.

Television is perhaps their greatest vehicle to indoctrinate your senses. When you consider that a brief, thirty-second commercial during the Super Bowl this year cost an incredible $5,500,000, it is easy to see why television is so successful in influencing the masses.

You know this to be true when you can recite the slogans and catchlines from the many commercials that you have seen throughout your lifetime.

"Where's the beef?"

"Just do it!"

"Built Ford tough."

"It's time to make the doughnuts."

Some of us can even sing along with the jingles!

"It takes two hands to handle a Whopper, the two-fisted burger from Burger King!"

"Give me a break, give me a break, break me off a piece of that Kit Kat bar."

"Like a good neighbor, State Farm is there!"

Television helps *program* us on which things we should eat, wear, and drive, while the music we listen to instills how we should feel about heartache and disappointment.

Titles like "Unbreak My Heart" by Toni Braxton, "Yesterday" by the Beatles, and "How Can You Mend a Broken Heart" by Al Green all address those sad occasions. I am sure you have your own favorites that immediately pop into your head whenever you are feeling down or unloved.

Even the cars we drive and the homes we live in are meant to be a reflection on how well we are doing. Life is not a game, so why are we keeping score? Yes! We are keeping score. You might not realize it because we do it without thinking about it.

When we compare what our neighbors have to what we have, we *are* keeping score. This is a dangerous practice. God has warned us about coveting that which belongs to someone else; it leads to sin. The beloved physician Luke tells us Jesus's words in Luke 12:15, "And he said unto them, Take heed, and beware of covetousness; for a man's life consisteth not in the abundance of the things which he possesseth."

When we hear about friends and colleagues going out to the theatre or concert, we begin keeping score.

"When am I going to get to go to a concert or an event? When is my turn?" We find ourselves suddenly reevaluating our life. We feel like we are missing out, and we need instant assurance that this is going to be rectified.

When I look at my aged car with its dings and dents and faded paint, I inevitably look across at my neighbor's shiny new car. I am keeping score, and he is winning!

But keeping score is not just about possessions and lifestyles. It is also about what we unconsciously keep track of in our relationships with others.

Far too many marriages are ruined because *of keeping score.* Here are a few ways that we hurt our relationships by playing this dangerous game.

"She doesn't dress up like other women!"

"He's letting himself go. Just look at that stomach!"

"She never supports my ideas."

"Just once, I wish he'd do something romantic!"

Thoughts like these are unfortunately commonplace in our relationships. And the misuse of social media has exasperated the situation. There are some social pages that you can join where the men or women just go to publicly criticize their spouses or boyfriend/girlfriends. This is a real shame, which only leads to destructive, relationship-killing feelings in all those who participate in it.

Jesus warns us in Matthew 7:5, "Thou hypocrite, first cast the beam out of thine own eye, and then shalt thou see clearly to cast the mote out of thy brother's eye."

The word *hypocrite* is derived from the Greek word meaning actor or pretender. Sometimes when we feel overly judgmental toward our partners, we should pause and examine our own behavior. We all can do a little bit better in many areas of our relationships. This should give us pause not to call out every flaw we see, since our own flaws may be much worse.

Keeping score is a losing game. Nobody wins! When we look at countless failed marriages, we hear how each person *kept score* on the failures of their partners.

"He never washed a dish. He just left it for me to do!"

This is a common complaint, which comes in many variations and is indicative of keeping score.

"He never cleans anything!"

"He leaves a mess everywhere, and I have to clean it up!"

"Would it kill him to pick those clothes up?"

"I have spent all day cleaning this house, and he didn't even notice it!"

And sometimes the complaints sound humorous, although the one complaining does not think they are funny at all.

"My goodness! What did he just do in this bathroom? Eww!"

"Really? You left one slice of bread in the bag?"

"He snored like a locomotive all night long, then asks me why I look so tired?"

This recalling of familiar complaints goes both ways, as you will soon see.

"Where is all this hair coming from?"

"If she makes creamed spinach one more time, I'm going to scream."

"When are you going to do the laundry? I need my favorite sweatshirt!"

"She won't watch any of *my* shows!"

"He *never* takes me out!"

When we were first married, we vowed to be united, *for better or for worse.* Why is it that now we often only think about the worst in each other?

We suffer from what researchers call the negativity effect. Simply put, this means that we have a built-in tendency to respond more strongly to negative events and feelings rather than good or favorable ones.

It is not that we do not see or notice the good our partners do; rather, when a negative situation is noticed, we tend to focus only on that one event. This negative bias is a real thing, and it can magnify every fault your partner has, making it seem that they cannot do *anything* right!

This negative outlook, fueled by the feeling of being unappreciated, will ruin a relationship. Keeping score will always lead to ill feelings that fester and cripple a loving union.

We cannot condemn our partners and love our partners at the same time. Focusing only on their faults and flaws will create an air of negativity. We need to be encouraging in our relationships. If one of you only hears about the wrongs you are doing, over time, you too will develop a negative outlook on your partner. Before long, you will be thinking, *What's the use?*

Take time to notice the little things your spouse does. Find things that deserve a compliment. Pick and choose the battles you want to bring to light. Forgive. Remember the reason you fell in love in the first place. Forgive.

There is another divisive problem we may encounter. This one has sprung up because of technology. It has brought with it an unforeseen culpability. I'm talking about our cell phones.

The problem is we don't talk, at least not to each other. Frequently in restaurants and other public places, we see husband, wife, and children, all engaged and engrossed with their phones.

Our phones have become a major obstacle for communication among married people and their families. Imagine that, an instrument that was created explicitly for communication has now become the nemesis for real conversation.

We play games on our phones, and we do research on our phones via the internet. We lose track of how much time our faces are planted in our phones, especially when we are on popular social media platforms like Facebook and Twitter.

Every post needs a like or a comment. Every opinion needs our comment as to why they are wrong. This all takes time, and it is taking valuable time away from our families. We need to start making a conscious effort to keep our phone use brief whenever we are in a family setting. Communication has always been the key to good relationships, and our spouses and children deserve to have our full attention when we are together. Time slips away fast enough without us ignoring each other for some trivial game or popular internet site. The family you save will be your own!

Keeping score in a relationship is a surefire way to ruin it. Talk it out. Don't shout it out. If there is something that is bothering you, don't keep it bottled up; bottled-up emotions have a way of exploding over time.

Turning to God's Word for some wonderful words for life will help keep you grounded in His love. We can find good advice from James 1:19, "My beloved brethren, let every man be swift to hear, slow to speak, slow to wrath;"

James is entreating us to respond in helpful and compassionate words. We must not speed up our mouths at the expense of slowing down our mind. Anger is a natural human response that everyone experiences. This emotion can be controlled, and when controlled, we exhibit faith in God, who is the one in control.

Or we can observe kingly advice from Proverbs 15:1, "A soft answer turneth away wrath, but grievous words stir up anger."

When people come to us in anger, we are often tempted to respond similarly—or even worse. Solomon suggests a better way to respond, with a soft answer. Lowering the volume of our voices, while taking the sharp edges away from our words, will defuse most situations, limiting the damage that could be done.

If life were truly a game, it would be God who set the rules. And winning would not be the goal for us; it would be to have fun playing it. God has set rules for humankind to obey, and they are meant to make sure we grow in our understanding and bring us closer to an intimate relationship with Him.

Just as our parents taught us rules to protect us from harm, so does our heavenly Father set rules based on His gracious love for us. That is what a good father does, and a good Father is what we have!

We have seen that keeping score is a detriment to our lives. The reason it is so damaging is that keeping score is me driven. It is silently placing your feelings and desires in a place of superiority over that of your partner. If you believe that you are the only one making concessions in your relationship, you will always see your partner as beneath you.

The answer is to give. Give until it hurts. No more keeping score. When we focus on which one of us is giving more to the relationship, we are in fact keeping score, turning our giving into taking or requiring. If we were giving freely of ourselves, we would be benefitting by the joy we felt each time we rose above the urge to keep score.

To give is to appreciate. Be attentive when your partner speaks to you, keeping eye contact so they are aware that you are really listening, and value their thoughts and concerns.

Regularly acknowledge what your partner does by offering your thankfulness that they do those things without hesitation.

Remember to notice and compliment the smaller things. Put an unexpected smile on their face.

Salvage those relationships while you still can. Through constant prayer, ask God to let you see the good things your partner does and to remember to express your appreciation for all that they do.

Joke with each other. Laughter is indeed the best medicine! When you mess up, make a joke about it. Don't become defensive. Proverbs 17:22 tells us, "A merry heart doeth good like a medicine, but a broken spirit drieth the bones." Laughing will certainly brighten your countenance!

Jay Leno once said, "You can't stay mad at somebody who makes you laugh." Some of the best times in my marriage with Fran came from our ability to laugh at ourselves. We have laughed until we cried over the dumbest things that we have done or said.

One time, when our best friends were over, Morgan was asked by her mom, Cindy, to get her a half glass of lemonade. I too had noticed that Cindy's glass was now empty and in need of ice as well. In a moment of obscurity, I blurted out, "Morgan, the ice is in the freezer!"

Where else would the ice have been kept? Hello, Mr. Obvious!

My concern was that Morgan might not put more ice in the glass and just fill it halfway with lemonade. It didn't come out that way, needless to say. My wife laughed so hard at my obvious blunder. We still laugh about it today.

Start laughing again in your relationships and put away the scoreboards. When we stress out about our circumstances, it does not make them go away; it only brings us more grief. Take heed to these wonderful words for life.

CHAPTER THREE

Have We Lost Our Kids?

Are we still able to train up our children, as the Bible suggests in Proverbs 22:6? "Train up a child in the way he should go and, when he is old, he will not depart from it."

Children are a gift from God. Although most Bible scholars translate *chanak* as the word *train,* meaning to initiate, there is also a translation of it as "to put something into the mouth." When we consider the infant child who must be spoon-fed to provide them nourishment, we can see the correlation with making sure our children, while young, get the biblical and moral food they need from their parents that will set them on the right path.

The problem with passing our faith and beliefs onto our children is twofold, time and distractions. Add this to the many mixed messages they hear at school and from our culture, and you have the makings for some mixed-up youth.

When I was a child, Sunday was reserved for Sunday school, church, and worship. Today, however, there are many things competing for our children's time and attention other than church.

Various types of sports, dance, music lessons, and other endeavors vie for our children's attentions. Many good parents *want* their children to be involved in these activities, but somehow, the once Saturday-only activities are now scheduled for Sundays as well. This places participation in such programs at odds with attending church and worship services. Hence why children participating in Sunday activities has almost vanished in contrast to the wants of other pursuits on Sunday mornings.

When will our children be properly taught what the Bible teaches if we do not set aside time for them to study? This is the great challenge today for parents and church ministry teams. Many children do not know the simplest things about the Bible, and because of this, they willingly accept the secular views on things like marriage and various lifestyle choices.

Our schools blindly teach evolution as fact, even though they have absolutely no example that they can prove. This teaching leaves little room for students to come to their own conclusion on how life came to be. Simply put, evolution cannot be observed. This makes the evolutionary theory just as faith based as our belief in intelligent design by our creator God!

If we fail to teach that God created the world and humankind, our children will not see the need to heed the words of the Bible. That being said, if God created the world as Genesis 1:1 proclaims, "In the beginning God created the heavens and the earth," then God gets to determine marriage and all other rules for humankind.

The secular world uses God as an afterthought, not the standard for behavior. Our politicians publicly profess faith in God while promoting abortion and the slaughter of millions of babies worldwide!

We must find the time to teach our children what faith in God really looks like. Moses told the Israelites how important this message was in Deuteronomy 11:18–20,

> Therefore shall ye lay up these my words in your heart and in your soul, and bind them for a sign upon your hand, that they may be as frontlets between your eyes. And ye shall teach them to your children, speaking of them when thou sittest in thine house, and when thou walkest by the way, when thou liest down, and when thou risest up. And thou shalt write them upon the doorposts of thine house, and upon thy gates.

This sounds rather important to me!

God is telling us three things we need to do. First, we must fill our hearts with the Word of God so that we can call upon its wisdom when we need it. Secondly, keep our eyes fixed upon the Word of God, making it always in the forefront of our minds.

And thirdly, let our tongues speak the truths of God's Word continually, particularly to our young children.

God wants us to read his Word, the Bible, and teach it to our children. There still is time to reintroduce our kids to God's Word, but it will take diligence and setting aside time to do it right. And just as important, we need to start this process early in our children's lives. By the time they are of the age of nine or ten, the ways of the world will strongly start to influence their opinions and beliefs.

One of the most important lessons a parent can pass along to their children is this: the Bible is not a myth; nor is it a book of stories. Let me give you an example of what I am talking about. Picture those cute arks that the secular world displays on their book covers concerning Noah and the flood. They commonly have cute animals all perched on top of an oddly shaped boat. This leads the children to believe it is just a story, like a fable, which really is not true. But teaching this same account as fact, with emphasis on God wanting to save Noah and his family, as well as all the creatures of the world, can make a huge difference how the children perceive and accept it.

There are even well intentioned Sunday school teachers who make the same mistake, calling them all Bible stories. It is better and more accurate to refer to them as biblical accounts.

"I am going to teach you today about a man called Noah. God used Noah to build a large ark that he and his family would use to save the animals, because a worldwide flood was coming! We can read about this account in Genesis chapter 6. An ark can also be described as a sacred chest that holds things of great value. God looked at Noah and his family and all the creatures of the world as valuable and worthy of saving." We should teach the account of Noah as history.

Jesus quoted the Bible as history many times. And He believed that the Old Testament was authoritative, decisive, and binding. Therefore, the Old Testament should be viewed as the Word of God in all that it says.

Jesus used it when he taught the crowds and again to defend His actions during His ministry. Scripture foretold His coming. We read about this in John 5:39, "Search the scriptures; for in them ye think ye have eternal life; and they are they which testify of me."

The people Jesus was addressing refused to believe in Him. You cannot convince someone who simply rejects the evidence they are provided. We teach our children so that they have a moral compass to follow, always in the light of God's Word. With scripture on His lips and history on His mind, Jesus was still rejected by the learned Pharisees.

Jesus spoke historically of biblical characters such as Adam and Eve. Here, in Matthew 19:4–6, Jesus describes God's plan for marriage by retelling this account. "Have ye not read that he who made them at the beginning, made them male and female; And said, 'For this cause shall a man leave father and mother, and shall cleave to his wife, and they two shall be one flesh?' Wherefore, they are no more two, but one flesh. What, therefore, God hath joined together, let not man put asunder."

Jesus addresses two Bible directives here. He shows that He believes in creation, by reiterating the Adam and Eve account.

And Jesus recounted God's original plan and view of marriage.
For all those who wonder what Jesus's opinion on marriage is,
this should set them straight.

Jesus referenced Noah in Matthew 24:37–39,

> But as the days of Noah were, so shall also the
> coming of the Son of man be. For as in the days
> that were before the flood they were eating and
> drinking, marrying and giving in marriage, until
> the day that Noah entered into the ark, And knew
> not until the flood came, and took them all away,
> so shall also the coming of the Son of man be.

This is warning us that when Jesus comes back, it will be
unexpected to those who are not watching for Him. Just as the
rains came suddenly and swept away a sinful world, those who
believe and are saved will be taken away suddenly, leaving behind
those who did not watch. It is speaking of the event we call the
Rapture.

Jesus also recalled Jonah while rebuking the Pharisees in
Matthew 12:39–41,

> An evil and adulteress generation seeketh after
> a sign, and there shall no sign be given to it, but
> the sign of the prophet, Jonah; For as Jonah was
> three days and three nights in the belly of the
> great fish, so shall the Son of man be three days
> and three nights in the heart of the earth. The
> men of Nineveh shall rise in judgment with this

generation and shall condemn it; because they
repented at the preaching of Jonah; and, behold,
a greater than Jonah is here.

To truly get our children interested in studying the Bible, we
need to show them how interesting it can be. Many books, plays,
movies, and songs contain phrases that are taken directly from
God's Word! We only need to make a list of such usage to inspire
a lively dialogue with our youth.

The geographical locations for many of the biblical accounts
are quite confusing, but if we find some maps of ancient Israel
and the surrounding countries, we can show how far men like
Paul traveled. We can use a modern map or globe to show them
what the areas look like today. Marking off the valley where
David faced Goliath, or showing them the Red Sea, which Moses
parted, will create great interest and discussion opportunities.

Ask them if they ever get into arguments with a sibling. The
Bible has many accounts of family members fighting. Jacob and
Esau would be a great example. There is also the account of
Joseph and his eleven jealous brothers who sold him into slavery!

You can even use current events to pique their interests.
Modern archaeology has found many important Bible time relics
that would fascinate the children. Brochures from museums offer
great pictures and descriptions of biblical pottery, jewelry, and
art. Match these up with Bible accounts, and the children will
be engaged.

Make sure you include the biblical characters who experienced
failures in their life, but with God's help they overcame them.

King David had Uriah murdered because he desired his wife, Bathsheba. Elijah lost confidence after his greatest victory because of the evil woman Jezebel. Saul persecuted the followers of Jesus ferociously, until he saw the light on the road to Damascus. There are so many great Bible accounts to choose from.

Teaching the Bible is a rewarding experience. Don't ever let them say that the Bible is boring, because it is anything but. We must strive to find new and exciting ways to teach our youth the importance of God's Word.

Tell them this then: the true purpose of studying the Bible is not so you can know more but that you will grow more in faith, in grace, and in hope. Those wonderful words for life need to be learned while they are still young!

> Christ, the blessed One, gives to all, Wonderful words of life. Listen well to the loving call, Wonderful words of life. All the wondrous story, Showing us His glory:
>
> Beautiful words, wonderful words, wonderful words of life. Beautiful words, wonderful words, wonderful words of life.

CHAPTER FOUR

Sin Has Left the Building

We live in a time where the word *sin* is seldom spoken of publicly. Today's preachers would rather speak of *love* than teach anything concerning sin. They choose to leave it up to God instead of calling out sin. Conformity to worldly beliefs and practices is destroying the church.

A pastor's calling is to shepherd their flock, which *is* their congregation. If they willingly avoid teaching about sin, they inherently leave their congregation to fall into sin.

As a shepherd, you would not lead your sheep toward anything dangerous. You would make sure you blocked their way, keeping them from danger. The congregation is your flock, and not warning them of sin (danger) is reckless as a called shepherd for God. By sidestepping sin and its punishment, you might as well lead the flock off a cliff!

Jesus spoke more about hell than he did about heaven. And he was quite descriptive in his words. We read about his warning in Matthew 13:41–42, where Jesus says,

> The Son of man shall send forth his angels, and they shall gather out of his kingdom all things that offend, and them who do iniquity, And shall cast them into a furnace of fire; there shall be wailing and gnashing of teeth.

So said Jesus, the man who loved us so much that He gave His life for us on Calvary. Jesus redeemed us, so we can trust that He would not deceive us with those words of torment and hellfire. They were not frightful images created to terrify the people. If Jesus spoke of hell, you can be assured hell is a real destiny. Jesus said in Matthew 11:15, "He that hath ears to hear, let him hear."

For what reason did Christ die on the cross? Was it not for the sins of the world? First John 2:2 states, "And he is the propitiation for our sins, and not for ours only, but also for the sins of the whole world!"

Here we see that Christ's sacrifice on the cross was sufficient to cancel the debt of our sins for all who come to faith in Him. Jesus is our substitute, bearing the punishment for our iniquities.

Using the Bible as the authority on sin, we see that Jesus, the apostles, and the prophets all listed the sins of the people multiple times, calling for repentance from them. Isaiah 59:2 warns us of the tragic nature of sin, "But your iniquities have separated between you and your God, and your sins have hidden his face from you, that he will not hear."

We are all called to repent throughout the Bible, but we are seldom reminded during the sermons. Acts 17:30 says, "And the times of this ignorance God overlooked, but now commandeth all men everywhere to repent."

Paul is speaking from Mars Hill, in the city of Athens. His good news for these Gentile intellectuals gathered there is that the "unknown god" being revered is the same God he is preaching about! He teaches them that idol worship must cease. The Gentiles could now be full fellow heirs with the Jews, through Christ's redeeming work.

Just like the term *sin*, we seldom hear anything about a need for repentance. John the Baptist preached the need for repentance, and he was the herald of Jesus. In Matthew 3:2, he said, "Repent; for the kingdom of heaven is at hand." There must be a *turning away* from our sins for true repentance to occur.

Even before he was born, Jesus was equated with saving us from sin. We read in Matthew 1:21, "And she shall bring forth a son, and thou shalt call his name Jesus; for he shall save his people from their sins." Jesus tells us likewise in Luke 19:10, "For the Son of man is come to seek and to save that which was lost."

God *still* knows the hearts of all people, and He is ever seeking to save those who are lost in their sins. Saved by grace through faith, many are led to salvation by trusting Christ. Jesus desires that *no one* falls by the wayside. Second Peter 3:9 declares, "The Lord is not slack concerning his promise, as some men count slackness, but is longsuffering toward us, not willing that any should perish, but that all should come to repentance."

There are many instances of Jesus speaking out about sin. The argument that Jesus would turn a blind eye to sin because of His loving nature is both wrong and insulting. We know that Jesus would not avoid those persons who were of desperate need of salvation. It was His grace-filled, three-year ministry's purpose to reach them!

One such example is when Jesus was being put to the test concerning a woman who was caught in the act of adultery. The account is found in John 8:1–11. The evil scribes and Pharisees had hoped to find fault in Jesus as they asked him what should happen to her. Jesus's response was to stoop down and begin writing in the sand, as if he had not even heard them.

There are many theories as to what exactly Jesus was writing. Could it be that he was writing down the sins of the accusers? Jesus knew what the scribes and Pharisees were doing. They had already disregarded the law by bringing the woman without the man. Justice was never their intention.

John 8:7 tells us, "So when they continued asking him, he lifted himself up, and said unto them, 'He that is without sin among you, let him first cast a stone at her.'"

Then Jesus stooped down again, writing in the sand once more. I believe that Jesus, this time, was commuting her sentence. After all, He is the ultimate judge.

In Mark 2:5, we see that Jesus forgave the sins of a sick palsy man by saying, "Son, thy sins are forgiven thee." Jesus further explains His right to do so in Mark 2:10, "But that ye may know that the Son of man hath authority on earth to forgive sins."

Yes, this statement is correct. Only God can forgive sins! Jesus is called *Son of man* almost ninety times, and most of those are by Himself. His miracle of healing the palsy man pointed to His power to forgive sins.

Back to our accusers and Jesus. Now after the men had heard what Jesus said, they were convicted by their own conscience, and each one—from the eldest to the last—went away. Jesus was now alone with just the woman. John 8:10–11 continues,

> When Jesus had lifted himself up, and saw none but the woman, he said unto her, "Woman where are those thine accusers? Hath no man condemned thee?" She said, "No man, Lord." And Jesus said unto her, "Neither do I condemn thee: go, and sin no more."

The last thing Jesus said is perhaps the most important thing, "Go and sin no more." Jesus was letting her know that He knew she was guilty. He was not overlooking her sin; he was simply showing her His divine grace and mercy.

Many people and church leaders use this story in a negative way. They claim that this account shows that we are not to judge. This is an error. The Bible clearly teaches Christians that we are to judge other believers and explains when and how to do it.

First Corinthians 6:2–3 clearly states,

> Do ye not know that the saints shall judge the
> world? And if the world shall be judged by you,
> are ye unworthy to judge the smallest matters?
> Know ye not that we shall judge angels? How
> much more things that pertain to this life?

This could be a message for us today as well. Paul is insinuating that we should stop living as if we are merely citizens of this world and its culture. We must live up to who we are in Christ, looking forward to the day we join Him forever! Those of us who keep His Word to the end are conquerors and can expect to share in authority over the nations.

And we are charged with judging fairly as well. Jesus tells us in John 7:24, "Judge not according to the appearance, but judge righteous judgment." Jesus said this because the religious Jews who were self-righteous could not look past the external when they ruled.

We learned long ago, in 1 Samuel 16:7, when God was choosing His king amongst Jesse's sons,

> Look not on his countenance, or on the height of
> his stature, because I have refused him; for the
> Lord seeth not as a man seeth; for man looketh
> on the outward appearance, but the Lord looketh
> on the heart.

John the Baptist judged. Jesus judged many times. He once called the Pharisees "a brood of vipers that had to escape being sentenced to hell" in Matthew 23:33. The entire Sermon on the Mount was a series of judgments condemning evil teaching practices. The apostles needed to judge the people for their actions. Paul said, "Know ye not that the unrighteous shall not inherit the kingdom of God? Be not deceived," concerning a laundry list of sins listed in 1 Corinthians 6:9! And Peter called out the false teachers, whom he rightly judged.

And finally, we live in a world where the question of sin has become entangled in a web of legalistic rhetoric, where people argue the virtues of their actions. Now there are no absolutes when it comes to sin anymore, since the culture embraces *whatever feels right* as the new standard.

Galatians 6:7 warns, "Be not deceived, God is not mocked, for whatever a man soweth, that shall he also reap." You cannot say that the preachers from the last two thousand years all got it wrong. We are living in the time of the church of Pergamum. The church at Pergamum was surrounded by a pagan culture, just like our increasingly godless country. Pornography, sex for sale, and other morally depraved issues defile our cities and the people who involve themselves with it. Churches are now changing their long-accepted guidelines for discipline in favor of culture-accepted ones.

John Wesley left a pearl of wisdom for us to ponder. He said, "Give me one hundred preachers who fear nothing but sin and desire nothing but God, and I care not whether they be clergymen or laymen, they alone will shake the gates of Hell and set up the kingdom of Heaven upon Earth."

We may have to live in this world, but we do not have to act like we belong to this world. When our churches start resembling the world more than our Lord, the price of ignoring sin is undeniable. More wonderful words for life to consider.

CHAPTER FIVE

Why Am I So Angry?

America is angry. We see it every day on our televisions and read about it on social media platforms. The fact that Americans are angry cannot be denied. The overwhelming evidence is damning.

But Christians are perhaps more noticeably angry. How can this be? If we are to represent Christ for the rest of the world, how can anger have taken control over us?

There are many reasons for this apparent migration toward rage. One thing that seems to stir up Christians from every denomination is our differences in theology.

Churches are being split over the interpretations of scripture. For many, it has become our focus, our Christian right to expose and argue with every post that bears any spiritual content.

Everyone sees things in a different light. This is what makes us unique. There will always be disagreements with interpretations of scripture. Where we are failing primarily is our public outrage. With searing rage, we viciously target political agendas without showing the mercy that Jesus inspired. Some posts that we have responded to bear no reflection of a loving Christian. The hate and anger in our words is so heavy-handed that it disqualifies our efforts.

Please do not misunderstand me. I am all about defending God's Word and will always call out the hypocritical and faith-damaging posts that would lead others astray. But even I have been guilty of speaking out with venom-laced words that have left me feeling ashamed.

The Christian ideals that I will always defend are the following: The Bible *is* God's Word, plain and simple, authenticated by the Holy Spirit. Jesus Christ is Lord and Savior and still the only way to heaven. In the beginning was God, and He is *the* Creator. Heaven and hell are real destinations because we are told about them by Christ Himself. Jesus believed the scriptures; why shouldn't I? Sin separates us from a holy God. Jesus is the Lamb of God who paid the penalty for our sins, thus freeing us from sin's power over us. And finally, I can do nothing without God.

Many people are angry because others let them down. We need to buffer our expectations of others or brace ourselves for constant disappointment. This includes family, friends, colleagues, and sometimes our church.

Failure in our own lives can be a huge reason for anger. Sometimes these failures are the fault of others, but more often than not, they are the result of something we did or did not do. Failures hurt us. If we don't properly come to grips with why we failed, it will stay with us, festering and piling up with other smaller failings until it becomes like a powder keg, ready to explode.

Sometimes we lie to ourselves. We do things that we might not want others to discover. Do you have a secret? Is this secret causing you distress, frustration, or guilt? Hiding these secrets can produce a great deal of anger.

Jesus is the picture of calm. Only a few times in scripture did we see him exhibit any type of anger other than righteous anger. I'm sure the moneychangers at the temple went home in shock that day, recalling his words and actions. As recorded in Matthew 21:12–13,

> And Jesus went into the temple of God, and cast out all them that sold and bought in the temple, and overthrew the tables of the moneychangers, and the seats of them that sold doves, and said unto them, "It is written, My house shall be called the house of prayer, but ye have made it a den of thieves."

Jesus's last words, "den of thieves," no doubt points to those who had been overcharging the visiting foreigners for sacrificial animals needed for temple worship. Moneychangers were needed because of the many types of currency being exchanged for temple currency. They may have also been taking advantage of the visitors with unscrupulous rates. Jesus chased them all out into the streets.

There is a wonderful hymn that talks about *peace like a river*. Isaiah 66:12 inspired it:

> For thus saith the Lord: Behold, I will extend peace to her like a river, and the glory of the nations like a flowing stream; then shall ye be nursed, ye shall be borne upon her sides, and be dandled upon her knees.

The powerful evidence that we are, indeed, walking in the will of God is the presence of peace in our lives. When we follow the path that God intended for us, we overflow with serenity. We would never experience true peace if we went our own way.

In Matthew 11:29, Jesus tells us, "Take my yoke upon you, and learn of me; for I am meek and lowly in heart, and ye shall find rest unto your souls." The peace He offers comes in waves. It does not mean that everything in your life will be calm and still, but rather, no matter where the ups and downs take you, there will be a peace that washes over you just as a river, allowing you to deal with whatever comes your way in faith. If God was with you when the sky was clear and sunny, trust that He will *still* be there when storm clouds arise.

Now that's *real peace*.

Brought to you by the Prince of Peace!

CHAPTER SIX

Fear Not

Fear can be paralyzing. Some Bible scholars say that the Bible tells us to *fear not* 365 times! That means every day of the year, you can read a verse encouraging you not to live in fear. God wants us to trust Him, and He has placed many reassuring verses in His Word for us to claim. Moses wrote in Deuteronomy 31:8, "And the Lord, he it is who doth go before thee; he will be with thee, he will not fail thee, neither forsake thee; fear not, neither be dismayed."

Anxiety disorders are the most common mental illness in the United States, affecting forty million adults. Those who suffer persistent anxiety can find it to be uncontrollable and overwhelming. Oftentimes, those who suffer from anxiety also find themselves in a state of depression.

God does not want us to suffer ill feelings. There are many verses in the Bible that can be encouraging words to those who suffer. First Peter 5:7 tells us, "Casting all your care upon him; for he careth for you." Indeed, God does care for you. Psalm 30:2 says, "O Lord, my God, I cried unto thee, and thou hast healed me."

David offered God immense thanks and grateful praise in this psalm for something he was suffering physically. We should always offer similar thanks in every area of our lives, not just when we are healed and strengthened.

Some of the most famous biblical characters suffered with anxiety: Martha, Job, Jonah, King David, Moses, and many more.

Remember the words Jesus said to Martha when she was complaining that her sister Mary was not helping her serve but was seated at the feet of Jesus, listening, as recorded in Luke 10:41,

> "Martha, Martha, thou art anxious and troubled
> about many things. But one thing is needful, and
> Mary hath chosen that good part, which shall not
> be taken from her."

Job felt the pressures of anxiety after he lost his family, his servants, his livestock, his wealth, and finally his health. We read in Job 2:9 that even his own wife questioned his remaining integrity as she told him to "Curse God, and die." And if that was not bad enough, we see that his three friends did not make him feel any better with their superficial assessment of him.

Jonah, who lived a life in fear of neighboring Assyria, fell into anxiety with the constant threat to his home and country. He welcomed the destruction of the people of Nineveh, feeling crushed when they repented and were spared by God, as detailed in Jonah 3:10:

> And God saw their works, that they turned from
> their evil way; and God repented of the evil that
> he had said that he would do unto them, and he
> did not.

King David displayed many symptoms of brutal anxiety, such as sleepless nights, fears, self-doubts, and crying. We know this because of the many psalms that he penned, whereby he mentions them. Psalms 31:10 is such an example: "For my life is spent with grief, and my years with sighing, my strength faileth because of mine iniquity, and my bones are consumed."

Moses, whom the Lord knew face-to-face, even suffered anxiety woes. When we analyze the things that happened in his life, we can see why. He was hidden as a baby and then cast in a river to save his life. He was raised by the daughter of Pharaoh. He was kept from his own people but witnessed their mistreatment and sorrows. He murdered a man to protect a fellow Hebrew. He was rejected by men when he tried to make peace between them. When his sin was discovered, he fled to a foreign land, and when God called him from the midst of the burning bush, he feigned inferiority, as recorded in Exodus 3:11, "And Moses said unto God, 'Who am I, that I should go unto Pharaoh, and that I should bring forth the children of Israel out of Egypt?'"

But perhaps one of the best examples of someone with anxiety was the account of Hannah, which is found in 1 Samuel 1 and 2.

There we are introduced to a man named Elkanah. First Samuel 1:2 says, "And he had two wives: the name of the one was Hannah, and the name of the other, Peninnah. And Peninnah had children, but Hannah had no children."

In biblical times, the most important contribution a woman could make to a household was to present her husband with children—in particular, a son. Failure to deliver on this obligation was often viewed harshly as a curse from God, bringing with it disgrace.

Now you can see just how terrible Hannah felt, but things got a lot worse. First Samuel 1:3 continues, "And this man went up out of his city yearly to worship and to sacrifice unto the Lord of hosts in Shiloh." We see that he would give Peninnah, his wife, and to all her sons and daughters portions of meat, while 1 Samuel 1:5 tells us, "But unto Hannah, he gave a worthy portion; for he loved Hannah: but the Lord had shut up her womb."

Now Peninnah would relentlessly provoke her about having no children. Year after year, Hannah had to endure this teasing whenever Elkanah went to make sacrifices at Shiloh.

Now Hannah, fully immersed in a state of anxiety and despair, wept bitterly and could not eat. Elkanah asked her why she wept and why she was not eating. He wanted to know why her heart was so heavy. Knowing that she grieved not having children, he said to her in 1 Samuel 1:8, "Am not I better to thee than ten sons?"

Hannah got up after they had eaten in Shiloh. First Samuel 1:10–11 says,

And she was in bitterness of soul, and prayed unto the Lord and wept bitterly. And she vowed a vow, and said, O Lord of hosts, if thou wilt indeed look on the affliction of thine handmaid, and remember me, and not forget thine handmaid, but wilt give unto thine handmaid a male child, then I will give him unto the Lord all the days of his life, and there shall no razor come upon his head.

And as she continued her prayer, Eli the priest noticed her mouth was moving. Hannah was broken as she spoke to the Lord from her heart, but, indeed, her lips were moving, and no voice was heard. Eli just assumed that she was drunk. First Samuel 1:14 tells us what happened next: "And Eli said unto her, 'How long wilt thou be intoxicated? Put away thy wine from thee!'"

But Hannah corrected him, saying that she had a sorrowful spirit and that she was just pouring out her soul before the Lord. Eli heard and believed her. First Samuel 1:17 says, "Then Eli answered and said, 'Go in peace, and the God of Israel grant thee thy petition that thou hast asked of him.'"

And immediately, Hannah went away, and she ate, and her demeanor improved since she was no longer sad.

That is how we should all be praying. We should be pouring out our hearts to the Lord in prayer. We underestimate prayer. We fail to give it our all, and we hold back our emotions. Hannah literally "cast her cares upon the Lord." Psalms 55:22 encourages us, "Cast thy burden upon the Lord, and he shall sustain thee; he shall never suffer the righteous to be moved."

The next day, Hannah and Elkanah rose early and worshipped before the Lord. When they had come home, Elkanah went into his wife, Hannah, and God remembered her.

First Samuel 1:20 details, "Wherefore it came to pass, when the time was come about after Hannah had conceived, that she bore a son, and called his name Samuel, saying, 'Because I have asked him of the Lord.'"

And when it was time again to offer sacrifice, Hannah stayed home to wean the child, while Elkanah went to Shiloh to worship.

Hannah planned on keeping Samuel until he was weaned, and then she would go and bring him, that he may appear before the Lord and abide there forever.

She asked God for a son and then gave him back to serve God. In 1 Samuel 2:1–10, we read Hannah's prophetic prayer. It is interesting to note that Mary, the mother of Jesus, would use words from Hannah's prayer in the prayer known as Mary's Song, the Magnificat, found in Luke 1:46–55.

Hannah had wept bitterly as she said her prayer, asking for a son. And the Lord listened. You know who else wept bitterly as He prayed? Jesus did. Listen to the words that can only be described as *agony in the garden*. This account is found in Mark 14:32–42:

> And they came to a place which was named Gethsemane; and he saith to his disciples, "Sit ye here, while I shall pray." And he taketh with

him Peter, and James, and John, and began to be greatly amazed, and to be very depressed; And saith unto them, "My soul is exceedingly sorrowful unto death; tarry ye here, and watch."

And he went forward a little, and fell on the ground, and prayed that, if it were possible, the hour might pass from him. And he said, "Abba, Father, all things are possible unto thee. Take away this cup from me; Nevertheless, not what I will, but what thou wilt."

And he cometh, and findeth them sleeping, and saith unto Peter, "Simon, sleepest thou? Couldest not thou watch one hour? Watch ye and pray, lest ye enter into temptation. The spirit truly is ready, but the flesh is weak."

And again he went away, and prayed, and spoke the same words. And when he returned, he found them asleep again (for their eyes were heavy), neither knew they what to answer him.

And he cometh the third time, and saith unto them, "Sleep on now, and take your rest. It is enough, the hour is come; behold, the Son of man is betrayed into the hands of sinners. Rise up, let us go; lo, he that betrayeth me is at hand."

This was the beginning of the most difficult time in Jesus's life. Jesus took His inner circle with him, Peter, James, and John, just as he frequently had. He expressed his sorrow to them, but they were still blind to what was about to occur. But Jesus was never alone. He had His heavenly Father in His thoughts and prayers.

Jesus did not just utter one prayer; He prayed three times. We are told He prayed so fervently that His sweat was like droplets of blood. The physician Luke confirms this in Luke 22:44, "And being in an agony, he prayed more earnestly; and his sweat was, as it were, great drops of blood falling down to the ground."

Jesus came to Gethsemane, troubled and sorrowful. He left there embracing his course, fortified in the truth of His mission. He embraced His destiny and His calling; He would be the obedient Son!

Like Hannah, Jesus's prayers were laced with his tears. Like Hannah, Jesus leaves Gethsemane a changed person, purposeful and focused. Like Hannah, God remembers Jesus and grants Him the courage to see things through.

Charles Spurgeon once said, "When you are so weak that you cannot do much more than cry, you coin diamonds with both your eyes ... The sweetest prayers God ever hears are the groans and sighs of those who have no hope in anything but his love."

Let Paul's words from Philippians 4:6–7 also encourage us:

> Be anxious for nothing, but in everything, by prayer and supplication with thanksgiving, let your requests be made known unto God. And the peace of God which passeth all understanding, shall keep your hearts and minds through Christ Jesus.

Hannah could not eat, and she cried often, but after pouring out her heart to God, she did eat, and her demeanor improved.

We can find peace in Christ! John 14:27 says, "Peace I leave with you, my peace I give unto you; not as the world giveth, give I unto you. Let not your heart be troubled, neither let it be afraid."

God encourages us to come boldly to the throne of grace when we pray. Take hold of God's promises. Let not your hearts be troubled.

Second Timothy 1:7 assures us, "For God hath not given us the spirit of fear, but of power and of love, and of a sound mind."

Remember these wonderful words for life. Memorize them, writing them on the walls of your heart and mind.

> Sweetly echo the gospel call, wonderful words of life, offer pardon and peace to all, wonderful words of life; Jesus, only Savior, sanctify forever.
>
> Beautiful words, wonderful words, wonderful words of life.
>
> Beautiful words, wonderful words, wonderful words of life.

CHAPTER SEVEN

Can I Trust the Bible?

Whenever anyone asks me why I trust the Bible, I simply tell them, "Jesus did!" Everything I believe has come from reading the Bible. I cannot separate the Old Testament scriptures from the New Testament writings. It is where I met Jesus. Through the history of the Jewish people, recorded in the Old Testament, I found the Messiah that was long promised.

With the first four words found in Genesis 1:1, "In the beginning God," I have accepted that we are here on earth because of an ever-present Creator God. I can say this because the Bible *begins* with God, not with a philosophic argument debating His existence.

Though science denies it, the proof of intelligent design is all around us and cannot be explained away. Archaeologists continue to unearth proof of biblical cities, biblical characters, and proof of many of the events that are recorded throughout the Bible.

In Jesus's day, the scriptures were the Old Testament. These writings were by men of various lifestyles—kings, scribes, shepherds. and prophets who wrote under the inspiration of the Lord Himself.

Jesus quoted from scripture some seventy-eight times. He dispatched Satan himself by correctly quoting three times from the book of Deuteronomy during his time in the desert, deflecting Satan's temptations.

Jesus referred to the Old Testament as the scriptures, the Word of God, and the wisdom of God. Jesus totally trusted the scriptures as truthful, and God-breathed. He told Satan likewise, in Matthew 4:4, "But he answered and said, 'It is written, Man shall not live by bread alone, but by every word that proceedeth out of the mouth of God.'"

The Old Testament speaks of Jesus's coming and predicts hundreds of events that come to fruition in the New Testament. Thereby, the New Testament testifies to the genuineness of the Old Testament, making both of these collections inseparably the Word of God!.

If Jesus is who He claims to be, then we must conclude that it was He who divinely inspired the writers of the Old Testament. If we declare that Jesus inspired it and quoted from it, He also authenticates it. This fact is vitally important considering the madness that some Christian leaders are considering these days.

There are those who believe that the church cannot grow any further because of its ties to the Old Testament. These same people foolishly suggest that we should not use it anymore. The argument goes people do not need to believe in the Old Testament to be saved, so let's do away with it and all of its controversial contents.

Jesus told us the Bible is true. If it is not, then Jesus was terribly wrong. If I learned about Jesus in the New Testament but am told the Old Testament is mainly myths and folk stories, why should I trust the things in the New Testament? This picking and choosing of what we should follow does nothing to inspire faith in the Bible.

There are even some pastors who only want to use Jesus's own words to validate salvation. Thomas Jefferson once thought that way, and he created his own version of the Bible that he cut and pasted, using only the teachings of Jesus. He simply ignored all the miracles and anything supernatural. What good was that? Did he have such doubt about the many miracles Jesus was credited for that it shook his faith? Or worse, was he ashamed of the things he omitted? I cannot say.

Jesus addresses unbelief in John 5:46–47, where he states, "For had ye believed Moses, ye would have believed me; for he wrote of me. But if ye believe not his writings, how shall ye believe my words?"

Moses wrote a great many things about the long-awaited Messiah. Jesus fulfills the description of the Passover Lamb. The blood He shed bought salvation for the world. Jesus is like the manna given to the Israelites every morning, for He is the

Bread of Life. When Moses asked God for water, a rock split open and quenched their thirst. Likewise, Jesus is the living water; if taken, He will quench your spiritual thirst forever. Moses spoke of God raising up a prophet as worthy as Himself. Jesus is clearly a luminary above!

We can plainly see that we are living in a post-Christian society. The signs are all around us. There is *no sin*, *every* lifestyle is blessed in God's eyes, hell is not real, and *all faiths* can eventually enter heaven. You can now represent yourself as male, female, or something entirely different! This makes the word *truth* totally negotiable!

I guess the preachers and Bible teachers for the last nineteen hundred years got it all wrong. At least that is what some progressive church leaders would have us believe. I have heard some pastors say, while holding up a Bible, "This is not God's Word!"

You might not need to believe that the Old Testament is true to be saved, but the Bible has got to be true for there to be *any* salvation. Jesus cannot be separated from the Old Testament simply because it is He who fulfills it!

Why is reading our Bibles so important? Most Christians know that reading God's Word is important. But far too many times, we get frustrated and confused, and very soon we set aside our Bibles for long periods at a time. We have no problem reading mainstream authors' new books cover to cover, but persistent study of God's Word seems to ever elude us.

Our spiritual well-being needs to be nourished by reading God's Word on a regular basis. Just as our bodies require good and wholesome foods to keep us of strong mind and body, so does our spiritual health need regular refreshment in the Word.

When we just look at the Bible, we can see the tremendous impact it has had on the world. The Bible was the first book ever to be printed. Since then, the Bible has become the most published and printed book in history. It has also been printed in just about every known language and dialect. It is an undisputed best seller year after year! Many households have more than one copy residing there.

Historically, many people have died horrible deaths in pursuit of ownership of their own copy. Throughout history, the Bible has been praised, cursed, banned, burned, restricted, and argued over. We swear not only *on it* but *at it* as well.

The Bible was translated into its present form painstakingly from the original languages, using verified ancient manuscripts. Men died to translate it into their own languages. It has been proven accurate to the smallest of details. It has been studied, dissected, and commentated on more than any book ever written.

The events found in this book have greatly influenced the art world as well. Countless paintings that reflect the many accounts found within the pages of the Bible are on display across the world in museums and art galleries.

It has been responsible for changing the lives of many over the centuries. People have found hope and reason to turn their troubled lives around. People have found peace and serenity by reading it faithfully and committing its words to memory.

Reading the Bible shows us God's character. If we have questions about God, this is where we will find the answers! Reading the Bible regularly also keeps us from sin. Psalm 119:1 says, "Thy word have I hidden in mine heart, that I might not sin against thee."

Paul warns us in Romans 12:2, "And be not conformed to this world, but be ye transformed by the renewing of your mind, that ye may prove what is that good, and acceptable, and perfect, will of God." We cannot expect to fight the false teachers of this world successfully when we do not know the truth contained in the Bible.

Then, in Hebrews 4:12, we see the ultimate power of the Word of God:

> For the word of God is living, and powerful, and sharper than any two-edged sword, piercing even to the dividing asunder of soul and spirit, and of joints and marrow, and is a discerner of the thoughts and intents of the heart.

This incredible cutting or piercing power of the scriptures is therefore like a surgical tool used to separate our deepest thoughts into good and evil. The Bible gives us everything we need to help us discern between the two.

God's Word is powerful and the ultimate authority. Jeremiah 23:29 confirms it: "Is not my word like a fire? saith the Lord; and like a hammer that breaketh the rock in pieces?"

The Bible is God's fire used to refine us. Its purpose is to purify us for service. Charles H. Spurgeon recalled, "I owe more to the fire, and the hammer, and the file, then to anything else in my Lord's workshop."

Yes! You *can* trust the Bible to be God's holy Word.

"The Bible is the only book where the author is in love with the reader" (anonymous).

CHAPTER EIGHT

False Teachers Offer Only False Hopes

I wrote a little about false prophets earlier. Let me explain how deceiving false prophets are and how easily you can be fooled and enticed by their promises and lies.

The Bible does not teach that God promises every Christian to be healthy and wealthy. There is also no *best life now* scenario while we live in this sin-filled world.

Second Timothy 4:3 tells us, "For the time will come when they will not endure sound doctrine but, after their own lusts, shall they heap to themselves teachers, having itching ears."

Second Timothy was the last epistle Paul would write. He was in a Roman prison, awaiting death. He could see the writing on the wall, that ravenous wolves in sheep's clothing would infiltrate the church and ravage his flock. He warned

Timothy to be on guard and watch for these treacherous false teachers. We too must keep our eyes and ears finely tuned to what is being put forth as gospel but in truth are only lies and empty promises.

We were warned that a time would come when people would follow preachers who tell them what they want to hear. That time is now! We are supposed to be seeking God's will. But instead, we are asking and expecting all our sickness to be wiped away and our bank accounts to be overflowing.

This creates great disappointment when the sickness and illnesses do not disappear and the financial windfalls never come. Why should we have expected these things when we are told clearly that we would experience tribulation in this life? We find in John 16:33, Jesus states, "In the world ye shall have tribulation: but be of good cheer; I have overcome the world."

It is an unfortunate reality that we all will face some type of crisis in our lives, whether it be health based or a financial crisis. No matter what kind of trouble we encounter, it can leave us frightened, alone, sad, or angry. Becoming a Christian doesn't make all of your troubles disappear; what it does do is give you an advocate in Christ to get through it.

The apostle Paul went further when he spoke of the trials we shall bear. In Romans 5:3–4, he says, "But we glory in tribulations also, knowing that tribulation worketh patience; and patience, experience; and experience, hope."

But here is the tragedy of the prosperity preachers. If you fail to be healed, if you fail to prosper, it is your lack of faith that prevented it! Imagine the crushed followers who felt they were doing everything right, and God was just saying, "No!"

These false preachers claim that dying on the cross, Jesus paved the way for all illnesses to be gone, and poverty shall be averted for believing Christians. This is just not so. There are many faithful Christians living in third world countries who have no chance for these false claims to ever come true. Sadly, they are casualties of the unscrupulous false preachers.

The false preachers outlandishly promote that Christian giving leads to overwhelming compensations from God. "Plant a seed!" is one of their favorite lines. They will also shout, "Write me a check right now for five hundred dollars. I feel a blessing coming on." But the worst one has got to be, "Money, money, money!" as they dance unashamedly before the people watching on TV.

We need only to give secretly, with a cheerful heart, to experience God's blessings. *Not* with the wrong motives of profiting, like you are buying a stock or a lottery ticket. God is not a genie, and you don't get three wishes.

The Word of Faith preachers tell a different lie. They teach that you can *claim it* if you *say it*, suggesting that the real power for health and wealth is in your mouth and the words you speak. *Star Wars* taught us that "the force is with you," but these modern-day false teachers push the belief in their own "force of faith."

They are so blasphemous they declare that the *faith force* operates independently from God Himself, and He is also subject to these laws. They are telling their followers that they are gods themselves!

They promote the same lie that Satan told Eve in the Garden of Eden. Genesis 3:4–5 says, "And the serpent said unto the woman, 'Ye shall not surely die; For God doth know that in the day ye eat thereof, then your eyes shall be opened, and ye shall be as God, knowing good and evil.'" We know how that worked out for Adam and Eve and the rest of humankind!

This is the main reason we were told in scripture to always test all things. First Thessalonians 5:21 says, "Prove all things; hold fast that which is good."

First John 4:1 warns us, "Beloved, believe not every spirit, but test the spirits whether they are of God; for, many false prophets are gone out into the world."

This is the reason we must read the Bible on a regular basis. We must search the scriptures, memorize the words, and use the "sword of the spirit" as well as the rest of the spiritual armor Paul advocates for in Ephesians 6:13–17.

We need only remember what the Lord said to Jeremiah when the false teachers arose. In Jeremiah 23:1–2,

> Woe be unto the shepherds who destroy and scatter the sheep of my pasture! Saith the Lord. Therefore, thus saith the Lord God of Israel against the shepherds who feed my people, Ye have scattered my flock, and driven them away, and have not visited them; behold, I will visit upon you the evil of your doings, saith the Lord.

And later in Jeremiah 23:16, we read,

Thus saith the Lord of hosts, "Hearken not unto the words of the prophets that prophesy unto you. They make you vain; they speak a vision of their own heart, and not out of the mouth of the Lord."

Take heed, Christian. Beware of the wolves in sheep clothing! They speak not wonderful words for life!

CHAPTER NINE

The Spirit Is Willing

Many people are confused about what or who the Holy Spirit is. Some think of the Holy Spirit as an elusive force, or some mysterious influence, or even some kind of substance that emanates from God the Father. He is so much more than that.

When a Christian becomes born again, they receive the gift of the Holy Spirit. The process begins when we fall on our knees and ask forgiveness for our sins. We then profess that Jesus Christ died on the cross to save us from our sins and that He rose again from the grave, victoriously, as the only beloved Son of God.

Paul assures us in Ephesians 2:8–9, "For by grace are ye saved through faith; and that not of yourselves, it is the gift of God—Not of works, lest any man should boast."

Grace is God's undeserved favor He bestows on believers as a blessing. It is unwarranted. No one has earned it. It is not ours because we were good. It is wholly God's gift to us. We have received it because God is good!

Jesus Himself received the Holy Spirit when He was being baptized in the Jordan River by John the Baptist. We read about this in Matthew 3:16–17,

> And Jesus, when he was baptized, went up straightway out of the water; and, lo, the heavens were opened unto him, and he saw the Spirit of God descending like a dove, and lighting upon him. And, lo, a voice from heaven, saying, This is my beloved Son, in whom I am well pleased.

Jesus first identifies the Holy Spirit as a "He" in John 16:13,

> When he, the Spirit of truth, is come, he will guide you into all truth; for he shall not speak of himself, but whatever he shall hear, that shall he speak; and he will show you things to come.

The Holy Spirit is a person, the "He" Jesus previously mentioned. He is also the third person of the Trinity. Though the Bible never mentions the word *trinity*, we read about this association in several places. One such instance is in Matthew 28:19, "Go ye, therefore, and teach all nations, baptizing them in the name of the Father, and of the Son, and of the Holy Spirit."

Romans 8:27 tells us that the Holy Spirit has a mind:

> And he that searcheth the hearts knoweth what is the
> mind of the Spirit, because he maketh intercession
> for the saints according to the will of God.

In Matthew 10:20, Jesus tells us that the Holy Spirit speaks. "For it is not ye that speak, but the Spirit of your Father who speaketh in you."

The Holy Spirit also teaches. We read Jesus's words, in John 14:26:

> But the Comforter who is the Holy Spirit, whom
> the Father will send in my name, he shall teach
> you all things, and bring all things to your
> remembrance, whatever I have said unto you.

The Holy Spirit can bear witness. We read in Acts 20:23, "Except that the Holy Spirit witnesseth in every city, saying that bonds and afflictions await me."

The Holy Spirit can testify. Jesus proclaims this in John 15:26:

> But when the Comforter is come, whom I will
> send unto you from the Father, even the Spirit of
> truth, who proceedeth from the Father, he shall
> testify of me.

The Holy Spirit helps humankind's infirmities. We see in Romans 8:26 the apostle Paul declaring,

Likewise, the Spirit also helpeth our infirmity; for we know not what we should pray for as we ought; but the Spirit himself maketh intercession for us with groanings which cannot be uttered.

The Holy Spirit oversees the shepherding of the church. Notice how He guides the church leaders in Acts 20:28:

Take heed, therefore, unto yourselves, and to all the flock, over which the Holy Spirit hath made you overseers, to feed the church of God, which he hath purchased with his own blood.

The Holy Spirit has the power to forbid. We read in Acts 16:6–7 that Paul and his companions had to change their plans:

Now when they had gone throughout Phrygia (which is Anatolia, Turkey) and the region of Galatia, and were forbidden by the Holy Spirit to preach the word in Asia, after they were come to Mysia (Northwest Anatolia), they attempted to go into Bithynia; but the Spirit allowed them not.

Paul knew better than to press the Holy Spirit.

The Holy Spirit can seal Christians. We learn in 2 Corinthians 1:21–22,

Now he who establisheth us with you in Christ, and hath anointed us, is God, who hath also

WONDERFUL WORDS FOR LIFE

sealed us, and given the earnest of the Spirit in our hearts.

The Holy Spirit worked in Christ's resurrection. We read about this in Romans 8:11:

> But if the Spirit of him that raised up Jesus from the dead dwell in you, he that raised up Christ from the dead shall also give life to your mortal bodies by his Spirit that dwelleth in you.

The Holy Spirit can be grieved. In the Old Testament, in Isaiah 63:10, we see, "But they rebelled, and vexed his Holy Spirit; therefore, he was turned to be their enemy, and he fought against them." It is far better to keep the Holy Spirit on *your* side.

The Holy Spirit should not be tested. Peter, addressing Sapphira, tells us in Acts 5:9, "Then Peter said to her, How is it that ye have agreed together to test the Spirit of the Lord? Behold, the feet of them who have buried thy husband are at the door and shall carry thee out."

The Holy Spirit can be both ignored and resisted. We see this in Acts 7:51, "Ye stiff-necked and uncircumcised in heart and ears, ye do always resist the Holy Spirit; as your fathers did, so do ye."

The Holy Spirit should *never* be blasphemed. A stern warning from Jesus, as we read His words in Mark 3:28–29,

> Verily I say unto you, All sins shall be forgiven unto the sons of men, and blasphemies with which

they shall blaspheme; But he that shall blaspheme against the Holy Spirit hath never forgiveness, but is in danger of eternal damnation.

This is the unpardonable sin!

Our human tendency is to try to fit everything we know about God into a small, tidy box that we can understand. But our awesome God is a wonderful mystery that requires us to search and seek out answers so that we can grow closer to Him.

It would seem that the only time we ever hear about the Holy Spirit is during the sermon on Pentecost Sunday. It is no wonder that all the things we have just learned seem so new to us. But we need to feel the tugging of the Holy Spirit on our lives, to guide us and direct us to do God's will.

Paul speaks of freedom in 2 Corinthians 3:17, "Now the Lord is that Spirit; and where the Spirit of the Lord is, there is liberty." This is the freedom from such things as sin, addiction, shameful desires, and more.

We know this by Paul's words in Romans 8:14–16:

> For as many as are led by the Spirit of God, they are the sons of God. For ye have not received the spirit of bondage again to fear; but ye have received the Spirit of adoption, whereby we cry, Abba, Father. The Spirit himself beareth witness with our spirit, that we are the children of God.

The Holy Spirit brings us deep peace, unexplainable joy, and a renewed passion for God.

The Holy Spirit is our guarantee of eternity through our salvation. In Ephesians 4:30, we read, "And grieve not the Holy Spirit of God, by whom ye are sealed unto the day of redemption." Nobody can take this away from you if you are truly saved.

The Holy Spirit is active and living within you. He helps you fight off the urges of this world. You can find strength in Him to defeat your demons. Paul teaches us in Galatians 5:16–17,

> This I say then, walk in the spirit, and ye shall not fulfill the lust of the flesh. For the flesh lusteth against the Spirit, and the Spirit against the flesh; and these are contrary the one to the other, so that ye cannot do the things that ye would.

It is The Holy Spirit who works to make God's Word come alive. He helps us worship God in spirit and in truth as we are required to do. In John 4:24, Jesus reminds us, "God is a Spirit; and they that worship him must worship him in spirit and in truth."

And finally, the Holy Spirit gives us gifts to be used to bless God and others. These gifts of the Spirit are gifts of grace granted by the Holy Spirit that are designed for the edification of the church.

The gifts are given, reflecting a believer's spiritual capabilities. They are word of knowledge, word of wisdom, gift of prophecy, gift of faith, gifts of healing, the working of miracles, discerning of spirits, speaking in tongues, and interpretation of tongues.

These are not to be confused with the fruits of the spirit, which are gradually developed as the believers abide in Christ and yield to the working of the Holy Spirit. There are nine in all: love, joy, peace, patience, kindness, goodness, gentleness, faithfulness, and self-control.

We are all unique. The gifts we receive reflect what the Lord requires from us. Every Christian should use the gift they have received to serve the Lord and others. But every Christian's goal should be to model the fruits of the spirit that make us Christlike. For us to dwell with Christ for eternity, we must exhibit all of these qualities. It is the purpose of our journey.

The Greek word translated *fruit* refers to the natural product of a living thing. Paul used the word *fruit* to help us understand the product of the Holy Spirit who lives inside every believer. This fruit of the spirit is produced by the Holy Spirit, not by the Christian! Like physical fruit needs time to grow, the fruit of the spirit will not ripen in our lives overnight. As we live the Christian life, we grow spiritually, acquiring these fruits as we are watered by the Spirit, through study of the wonderful words for life.

Do you know your gift? Have you been using it to the glory of God?

CHAPTER TEN

Worship God with Your Awe

Jesus tells us in John 4:24, "God is a Spirit; and they that worship him must worship him in spirit and in truth."

The Old Testament Hebrew word for worship is *shachah*, which translates "to bow before and prostrate yourself." Lying flat on the ground before your God shows real reverence for him!

The appropriate response when coming into the presence of the Lord is awe. Isaiah saw the Lord sitting on a throne and cried out, "Woe is me! For I am undone, because I am a man of unclean lips" (Isaiah 6:5). Isaiah was in awe of God Almighty.

The New Testament equivalent word for worship is *proskyneo*, which is understood to mean "to fall upon the knees and touch the ground with the forehead as an expression of true reverence."

Psalm 95:6 says, "Oh come, let us worship and bow down; let us kneel before the Lord our maker."

Psalm 132:7 states, "We will go into his tabernacles; we will worship at his footstool." During his three-year ministry, many thankful, aw-struck people fell at the feet of Jesus. Here is a list of people whose lives were changed forever after showing Jesus their reverence for him: the wise men fell at baby Jesus's feet, Jairus the synagogue ruler, the Syrophencian woman whose daughter had an unclean spirit, the man possessed by Legion, the woman who but touched his hem, Mary of Bethany, the leper who had returned to give thanks, and many more.

When most people think about worship, they often mention the word *praise.* They have the wrong idea that praise is just the same as worship. Praise, simply put, is thanking God for all the things He has done in our lives. Praise goes hand in hand with *thanksgiving.* It is our expression of admiration and approval. Worship is much more!

Worship is when we elevate something or someone, placing it or them on a sky-high level. We need to worship God not just for the things he has done but for who he is: the Creator and our Father who art in heaven.

Only those who are truly born-again believers can worship in spirit and in truth. It happens when our spirit connects with God's Spirit. We must remember that God is holy and not just one of the boys when we come into His presence.

When we look at Psalm 96:9, we note, "Oh, worship the Lord in beauty of holiness; fear before him, all the earth." In some translations, the word *fear* is replaced with *tremble*. We should indeed tremble before the awesomeness of God!

We are warned in Proverbs 9:10, "The fear of the Lord is the beginning of wisdom and the knowledge of the Holy One is understanding." This is not meant to scare us but rather to let us always remember God's greatness. It fosters a continual awareness of Him and the need for our reverence and obedience.

When we look at something spectacular like the Grand Canyon, we might tremble at the view because it too is awe inspiring and, depending upon where you are standing, quite dangerous as well.

So, fear and trembling can be equivalent to awe, the feeling of great wonder and reverence. Awe of God correctly expresses our love of God. The Christian life is a love relationship with God!

This is the reason Jesus tells us in Mark 12:30, "And thou shalt love the Lord thy God with all thy heart, and with all thy soul, and with all thy mind, and with all thy strength: this is the first commandment."

The most powerful worship service is one that is predicated on God's Word. When we are moved with emotion because of the awe-inspiring words that stir our hearts, we have made the connection and have moved much closer to our heavenly Father.

It is truth we must find, not a desire to feel good or experience entertainment that makes us worship Him. It is the Holy Spirit who is always in charge of a good worship service! It is about glorifying Jesus and taking on His nature, stifling the worldly noise, and focusing on Him and Him alone.

You should come to worship expecting to encounter God! In Matthew 18:20, Jesus tells us, "For where two or three are gathered together in my name, there am I in the midst of them."

OK. The Holy Spirit will orchestrate the worship. What must we bring to it? What we need to bring can be found throughout the scriptures. Psalm 100, for example, gives us clear directives to accomplish this task.

First, we must come together as a family, the family of God. When I taught adult Sunday school, we would sing hymns before we began our studies. Inevitably, the song "The Family of God" by William J. Gaither would be requested.

> I'm so glad I'm a part of the family of God—I've been washed in the fountain, cleansed by His blood! Joint heirs with Jesus as we travel this sod, For I'm part of the family ... the family of God!

Those are truly great words to get us in the right spirit to sing praises to God. Just more wonderful words for life. And that's why Psalm 100 is a great starting point for worship. It begins, "Make a joyful noise unto the Lord, all ye lands. Serve the Lord with gladness; come before his presence with singing" (Psalm 100:1–2).

Are you in the right frame of mind when you come to worship? Have you set your worldly concerns aside and focused on the job at hand, praising God and worshipping our Creator?

You cannot be looking at your phone. You cannot be going over a shopping list in your head that you plan on completing after the service. You cannot be dreading the wash that has been piling up over the week and is sitting in the basement, just waiting to be put into the machine.

You are here for one reason at this one time of the week, to truly worship the Lord. A clear mind must be established to begin worshipping properly. Leave your worldly baggage at the door.

And remember, we are here to *sing out,* not just coast through the verses unenthusiastically. We need to make that joyful noise that God is expecting. The Israelites would *shout* their praises to God. We should do no less, singing with passion and a joy-filled countenance.

God knows most of us do not sound like Whitney Houston. But he does expect us to put our hearts into it. Our faces should reflect the joy of praising God through song—not like we need another cup of coffee to get us through the service!

My wife and I have a little disagreement concerning the art of singing. I once told her that angels do not sing; they speak or chant but do not sing. She thinks I'm nuts!

When we search the scriptures, most times, when angels are mentioned, they speak words that we just assume are being sung.

Take the popular Christmastime reading found in Luke 2:13–14,

> And suddenly there was with the angel a multitude
> of the heavenly host, praising God, *and saying*
> "Glory to God in the highest, and on earth, peace,
> goodwill toward men."

See? No singing! The angels merely spoke those words.

My point is, that God has gifted humankind to be able to sing because He has provided the world salvation through his Son, Jesus Christ. That is a real reason to sing!

The angels do not need salvation, so they do not need that emotional connection that singing brings us. That is what makes our songs of praise so special. So, when you are at worship, sing like it is your special gift back to God! Since it is.

As the redeemed of God, we are His property. First Corinthians 6:20 states, "For ye are bought with a price; therefore, glorify God in your body and in your spirit, which are God's."

Psalm 100:2 goes on to say, "Serve the Lord with gladness." We have been purchased with Christ's blood. We are to serve willingly, obediently, and without question.

How are you serving the Lord? You can serve Him in a variety of ways, through prayer, through stewardship, through teaching, and so on. God can use all of you. He has done it with many people before you. Do not think that He cannot grow your mustard seed into a mighty tree.

It is so important for today's Christian to know whom we serve. This can be a painful eye-opener for many. We are to be wholly committed to the Lord. A question that we can ask ourselves will reveal a lot about who or what we really serve.

Our God is whatever we give the most time, resources, or thoughts to. Whatever we are consumed with, that is our God. It can be humbling to truthfully answer this question. Of course, our spouses and families are most in our thoughts, but God desires to be first. His promise to provide for us and protect us is why.

This is our perfect sacrifice that we bring to God—our lives, dedicated to service and witnessing for Christ who redeemed us!

This, my friends, is worshipping in spirit and truth—when we give our all to the God who saved us from our sins.

Zephaniah 3:17 confirms it:

> The Lord, thy God, in the midst of thee is mighty; he will save, he will rejoice over thee with joy; he will rest in his love, he will joy over thee with singing.

Did you hear those wonderful words for life? God sings over us! I didn't hear any angels singing ...

CHAPTER ELEVEN

Free to Forgive

Can you think of all the times you have done something you regretted? Of course not. We have all spent a lifetime hurting and being hurt by friends, family members, spouses, coworkers, and more. Many of the times, it was unintentional. But sometimes it was not.

Asking someone for their forgiveness can be uncomfortable. But if we don't seek forgiveness for our transgressions, we have a real chance of losing the person we wronged. It happens all the time. Families and friendships are permanently fractured.

Then there are those people who have done you wrong. It is amazing that people can hold a grudge against their own family members. You know plenty of stories about family get-togethers that need to be well thought out, so that certain siblings or relatives are seated at the other end of the table at Thanksgiving dinner. Let's try to keep them from tossing the mashed potatoes and stuffing!

The Bible has plenty to say about forgiveness—and for good reason. To forgive is an act of love. Jesus schooled Peter concerning how often to forgive in Matthew 18:21–22.

> Then came Peter to him, and said, Lord, how often shall my brother sin against me, and I forgive him? Till seven times? Jesus saith unto him, "I say not unto thee, until seven times; but, until seventy times seven."

Jesus was illustrating how important it is for us to always forgive our brothers and sisters. No keeping score!

In Matthew 6:9–13, Jesus was teaching the disciples how to pray. He included the statement "forgive us our debts, as we forgive our debtors." And immediately after the *amen* of the Lord's Prayer, Jesus addresses forgiveness yet again.

Here in Matthew 6:14–15, Jesus says,

> For if ye forgive men their trespasses, your heavenly Father will also forgive you; But if ye forgive not men their trespasses, neither will your Father forgive your trespasses.

We need to confess our sins daily in prayer. First John 1:9 instructs us, "If we confess our sins, he is faithful and just to forgive us our sins, and to cleanse us from all unrighteousness." Why should we do this?

Everyone needs a vibrant relationship with God. John speaks about this fellowship in 1 John 1:5–8:

> This, then, is the message which we have heard of him, and declare unto you, that God is light, and in him is no darkness at all. If we say that we have fellowship with him, and walk in darkness, we lie, and do not the truth; But if we walk in the light, as he is in the light, we have fellowship one with another, and the blood of Jesus Christ, his Son, cleanseth us from all sin. If we say we have no sin, we deceive ourselves, and the truth is not in us.

Through the Bible, the Word of God, the indwelling Holy Spirit shows the Christian that he still possesses an old nature and needs forgiveness of his sins. Sin interrupts our fellowship with God, but it can never change our saved relationship with Him. Our confession, through prayer, restores fellowship with God instantly, keeping our fellowship unbroken.

The apostle John continues his good news in his next chapter. First John 2:1–2 declares,

> My little children, these things write I unto you, that ye sin not. And if any man sin, we have an advocate with the Father, Jesus Christ the righteous; And he is the propitiation for our sins, and not for ours only, but also for the sins of the whole world.

I cannot help but think of the hymn we all know so well, "Jesus Paid It All" by Elvina M. Hall. The refrain goes like this: "Jesus paid it all, All to Him I owe; Sin had left a crimson stain— He washed it white as snow." Those are more wonderful words for life!

Forgiveness is not always needed just for something we did; sometimes it is for something we failed to do. Either way, the guilt we feel can hold us accountable for a lifetime. Failing to forgive *ourselves* for past mistakes in judgment is life altering. Shame and blame can weigh a person down, stifling any kind of life.

This kind of nontherapy pushes us away from fellowship with God. We have an obligation to forgive. Remember what Jesus said, "*Seventy times seven.*" Saying "I will never forgive myself" is denying the sin.

What we really cannot believe is that we did the offense in the first place! It hurts our pride. It makes us relive the situation over and over. We desperately want to discover the *real* culprit. But it is always the same though. The culprit is sin. And that's OK. Remember, we have an advocate in Jesus.

Self-forgiveness is an important part of our own self-evaluation. We cannot go forward if we refuse to honestly regard our transgressions as sin, caused by our sinful nature.

News flash: we aren't perfect. Only one man walked this earth sinless, and that man was Jesus Christ.

Many times, when we fail to forgive others, it is like we are covered in chains, dragging the injustice around everywhere we go.

Notice how I said *we are covered in chains*. Waiting for someone to apologize to us can be futile. Oftentimes, the person who wronged us seems unaffected by the transgression. They don't mention it or seem ashamed of it in any way. Why should you carry such a burden that only you are suffering from?

We should heed the words of Saint Augustine, "Resentment is like taking poison and hoping the other person dies."

Enough is enough!

It's time to forgive and break the chains of hostility. Free your mind, take out the trash, and start living again. Resentment will age you. Why should you let someone else have such a large piece of real estate in your head?

Forgiving someone their wrongs unshackles *you*. And it does not mean that you are letting someone else get away with something. It is making the right choice to let go of hurtful feelings that only hurt you.

Unforgiveness can be a dark and lonely prison in which you hold the key as chief jailer. Once you forgive, you allow the wounds that you have endured to heal. Unforgiveness just fills us with rage and bitterness. You hold the key; unlock the chains and free yourself. Forgive.

Forgiving doesn't make the offense any less. Psalm 56:8 reminds us that God collects every tear we shed and records all of our sorrows. We must remember that we live in an imperfect world with imperfect people. Disappointments and hurt feelings as well as all kinds of betrayals can be unavoidable. Extending forgiveness honors and glorifies God; an unforgiving heart does not.

Learning to forgive others just as God forgives helps us grow and mature into a contented and joyous person. Perhaps the best example of forgiveness comes from reading about Joseph forgiving his brothers, who many years earlier had sold him into slavery.

Joseph had suffered many things since his brother's betrayal, including prison. But because the Lord was with him, Joseph prospered as well. And he eventually rose to a position of power and authority under Pharaoh.

He could have paid back his brothers by making them slaves or even executing them as spies. But Joseph was compassionate. He also saw that God had used their crime to help a great multitude, including his own wayward brothers.

Genesis 50:20 records Joseph's realization of the effect of his brother's transgression: "But as for you, ye thought evil against me; but God meant it unto good, to bring to pass, as it is this day, to save many people alive."

Do not be like those who take their unforgiveness to the grave. Forgive!

Harriet Beecher Stowe, the gifted author an abolitionist, once said, "The bitterest tears shed over graves are for words left unsaid, and deeds left undone." Forgive!

Forgiveness exudes grace, and God's grace is unmatched. Forgive!

Psalm 103:12 says, "As far as the east is from the west, so far has he removed our transgressions from us." Forgive!

Unchain yourself. Then give it all to God.

In Matthew 11:29–30, Jesus said, "Take my yoke upon you,

and learn of me; for I am meek and lowly in heart, and ye shall find rest unto your souls. For my yoke is easy, and my burden light."

Jesus paid it all, all to Him I owe, sin had left a crimson stain—He washed it white as snow.

Forgive!

CHAPTER TWELVE

We Fail to See

Everyone has failed at something. Failing hurts. It is embarrassing when we fail. We want to keep our failures a secret so that nobody finds out about them. But wise people learn from their mistakes, their failures. You should not be labeling yourself as a loser. You may have tried something and failed, but you only become a failure when you quit, give up, or stop trying.

The Bible is filled with wonderful words for life. Psalm 73:26, reads, "My flesh and my heart fail, but God is the strength of my heart, and my portion forever."

There will be times of failure in our hectic lives, but it is the Lord who will sustain us whenever we find ourselves in the deepest, darkest caverns of despair. He is the rock of our hearts, the cornerstone of our faith.

Proverbs 24:16 ensures us, "For a just man falleth seven times, and riseth up again." Though we may fall through failures of our own, we are never crushed because the Lord upholds us with His mighty hand.

When we look at failures in our lives, the spectrum is vast. We may consider ourselves a failure for any of the following life experiences: our failed relationships, we experimented and got hooked on drugs or alcohol, we committed a crime or were arrested, we cannot keep a job, we *think* that we are bad parents, we failed to get a good education, we are not successful in many things we attempt. Of course, this list is brief. It is only meant to show a wide disparity of possible things we can fail at. Failures that are not mentioned here are just as devastating as the ones mentioned.

There are many people in the Bible who experienced failure. We know many of them as Bible heroes. From Noah to Peter, the Bible is filled with accounts of people making mistakes and still going on to greatness as instruments of God. God is in the business of retooling His people so that they can serve Him better!

In Hebrews 11:7, we see,

> By faith Noah, being warned of God of things not seen as yet, moved with fear, prepared an ark to the saving of his house, by which he condemned the world, and became heir of the righteousness which is by faith.

Noah will be forever remembered as one of the greatest Bible heroes for his unwavering faith in building an ark as the Lord had instructed him. After the Flood, through his family of eight, the world was given a fresh start, and the animals were saved to multiply across the world.

Noah's failure came after they had exited the ark and while they were building a new world. Many people in the Bible had failed miserably before Noah did but none more epically! Noah's moral failure of drunkenness led to a shattering effect on his family's tranquility. It also led to Ham's descendants becoming slaves of Noah's other two sons' lineage. Wars and constant enmity then consumed Noah's descendants for thousands of years. All of this because he allowed himself to be discovered naked and drunk.

Peter, Peter, Peter. Where shall we begin? One of the greatest disciples and apostles to ever follow Jesus had his fair share of failures in his lifetime. But Jesus saw fit to keep him in His inner circle along with James and his brother John. Jesus reacted to Peter's failures with goodness and patience, always ready to welcome him back after one of his misgivings.

Peter's most unforgettable failure was when he failed to *continue* his walk on the water across the Sea of Galilee. Peter stepped out of the boat in faith, his feet standing firmly atop the water. Then without hesitation, Peter began walking toward the Lord Jesus. What a miracle! Then, suddenly, Peter took his eyes off Jesus, and fear overtook Peter. For now, he could only see the winds and the violent waves surrounding him. And as he began to sink into the sea, panicking, he cried out, "Lord, save me." Then immediately Jesus stretched forth His hand and caught him. And Jesus said in Matthew 14:31, "O thou of little faith, why didst thou doubt?"

Another failure came when Peter could not stay awake when Jesus needed him the most in the Garden of Gethsemane. Jesus had been praying three different times, and each time, Peter and the other disciples were fast asleep instead of keeping watch. Jesus had been sweating droplets of blood, filled with sorrow over what was soon to take place. In Matthew 26:41, Jesus tells us, "Watch and pray, that ye enter not into temptation; the spirit indeed is willing, but the flesh is weak."

And yet another failure for Peter occurred on a mountaintop. Peter foolishly interrupts Jesus on the Mount of Transfiguration while He is speaking with Moses and Elijah. He suggests that they build three booths for shelter, one for each of them. Peter does not realize his error of placing Jesus on the same level as Moses and Elijah. Jesus is far above!

I am going to stop picking on Peter but not before I mention this last failure. His denial of Jesus three times! It is hard to believe that someone as strong-willed and outspoken as Peter could deny his friend and teacher with whom he had spent the last three years! But he did. Jesus told him that he would. We read in Matthew 26:33–34,

> Peter answered and said unto him, Though all men shall be offended because of thee, yet will I never be offended. Jesus said unto him, "Verily I say unto thee that this night, before the cock crows, thou shalt deny me thrice."

When Jesus had been taken away to be questioned by the high priest Caiaphas, Peter followed at a distance to see what was going to happen. We read about this in Matthew 26:69–75:

> Now Peter sat outside in the court, and a maid came unto him, saying, Thou also wast with Jesus of Galilee. But he denied it before them all, saying, I know not what thou sayest. And when he was gone out into the porch, another maid saw him, and said unto them that were there, This fellow was also with Jesus of Nazareth. And again he denied with an oath, I do not know the man. And after a while came unto him they that stood by, and said to Peter, Surely, thou also art one of them; for thy speech betrayeth thee. Then he began to curse and to swear, saying, I know not the man. And immediately the cock crowed. And Peter remembered the words of Jesus, who said unto him, Before the cock crows, thou shalt deny me thrice. And he went out, and wept bitterly.

Those have to be some of the saddest words ever written in the Bible. "And Peter remembered the words of Jesus." After this, Peter went out and wept bitterly! Can you blame him?

There are other Bible characters who failed, yet God used them for good. Moses murdered a man and buried him in the sand, defending one of his Hebrew brothers. God used Moses to free the Israelite slaves from Pharaoh of Egypt and to later to write the Pentateuch, the first five books of the Bible, also known as the Torah.

God chose David as a young man to be his king over Israel. In 1 Samuel 13:14, we see why: "The Lord hath sought him a man after his own heart." Yet David would later have sex with a married woman he saw bathing from his rooftop. If that was not bad enough, when Bathsheba became with child, he conspired to have her husband killed in battle to hide his sin.

David also had troubles being a good parent. And these troubles escalated into a war between brothers. Amnon had violated his half-sister Tamar sexually. Tamar's full brother Absalom finds out and despises him for it. David is aware that the incident took place, but rather than address it like a good father, he chooses to ignore it. Two years pass by, and Absalom and Amnon go into the country on a trip. Absalom entices Amnon with wine and eventually has his servants slay him while drunk. A civil war broke loose among the two factions, including David's family members, nobles, and many members of the army. People died. Absalom grew to hate David, vowing to take away his father's kingdom. In the end, David lost both sons and friends and loyal servants in the fray.

Then we have the strongest man to ever walk the earth, Samson. He was a gift of God to his parents, Manoah and his barren wife. An angel of the Lord brought news that she would bear a son and he was to be treated as a Nazirite, who could not set a razor to his scalp. Samson grew, and the Lord blessed him.

But Samson yielded to temptations, visiting the evil cities of the Philistines. He once killed a lion on the way there, when the

Spirit of the Lord came upon him, simply tearing it in two. When he returned, he looked for the carcass of the beast, and when he had found it, there was a swarm of bees and much honey inside the carcass. He took some and ate it, also giving some of it to his parents. But he did not tell them it came from the carcass of the lion. This was for good reason. It was a sin for him to touch or go near anything that was dead. He defiled himself, and his parents were defiled, although they were not aware of it. These are the kinds of failures Samson regularly engaged in. He drank strong wine, he touched dead things, and he mingled with the enemy and their women.

But God still used Samson to weaken the Philistine nation. He was a judge over Israel for twenty years. He hurt himself as well as others with his reckless behavior. But he is regarded in the book of Hebrews as a hero of the faith.

Though he was betrayed by Philistine women twice, he will end his life in God's favor. We all know the account of Samson and Delilah. How she tricked him for much silver. How the Philistines would gouge out his eyes and fasten him to millstones, forcing him to grind meal like a beast. And how God gave him back his strength to pull down the house by breaking the pillars that supported it, killing thousands of Philistines in the process.

There are so many more examples of people with problems who God elevated in His service. The Bible is filled with these wonderful words for life, where no one is too bad, or too small, or too old to fulfill God's plans.

Paul encourages us in Philippians 4:13, "I can do all things through Christ, who strengtheneth me." This is one of those verses that you can emphasize each word in the verse to make it sound more powerful of a promise!

"*I* can do all things ..."

"I *can* do all things ..."

"I can *do* all things ..."

I think you get the idea. Just more wonderful words for life!

God wants to help you wherever you are—confused, unsure, beaten down, brokenhearted, and desperate. Isaiah 41:13 says, "For I, the Lord thy God, will hold thy right hand, saying unto thee, Fear not; I will help thee."

There are no failures you cannot rise above with God on your side. There is no hill too high or valley too wide that God cannot help you cross. Turn your failures over to Him in prayer. Ask for guidance, ask for patience, ask for vision to see things through.

When we consider our failures as lives lost, we must remember the lesson we learned in Jeremiah 18:1–6:

> The word which came to Jeremiah from the Lord, saying, Arise, and go down to the potter's house, and there I will cause thee to hear my words. Then I went down to the potter's house, and, behold, he wrought a work on the wheels. And the vessel that he made of clay was marred in the hand of the potter; so he made it again another vessel, as seemed good to the potter to make it. Then the word of the Lord came to me saying, O house of Israel, cannot I do with you as this potter? Saith

the Lord. Behold, as the clay is in the potter's
hand, so are ye in mine hand, O house of Israel.

We fail to see. We fail to see that God has always and will
always be there, just when we need Him. We fail to see the
possibilities that only God can allow to happen. In the hands of
our heavenly potter, we can be reshaped. We can be molded into
the vessels that God requires. We may think our plans are too
grandiose, but God's plans are bigger!

I leave you with these wonderful words, as recorded by
Jeremiah in Lamentations 3:22: "The steadfast love of the Lord
never ceases; his mercies never come to an end."

Beautiful words, wonderful words, wonderful words of life,
Beautiful words, wonderful words, wonderful words of life.

NOTES

All of the scriptures used were taken from the New Scofield Study System Bible KJV.

Commercials cited for familiarity: Wendy's 1984 commercials, Nike's 1988 commercials, Ford 1979 commercials.

Recording artists mentioned: Toni Braxton's 1996 *Secrets* album; the Beatles' 1965 *Help!* album (the Silver Beetles); and Al Green's 1972 *Notting Hill* album.

Statistics about anxiety taken from World Health Organization figures.

"Wonderful Words of Life" song taken from *Hymns for the Family of God*, Paragon Associates, Inc. Written in 1874 by Philip P. Bliss

"The Family of God" song taken from *Hymns for the Family of God,* Paragon Associates, Inc. Written in 1970 by William J. Gaither.

Printed in the United States
by Baker & Taylor Publisher Services